Goals

Bucket List

Inspirational Quotes

Money

Relationship

Wellbeing

Career / Education

Goals

Bucket List

Inspirational
Quotes

Money

Relationship

Wellbeing

Career / Education

Goals

Bucket List

Inspirational Quotes

Money

Relationship

Wellbeing

Career / Education

Goals

Bucket List

Inspirational
Quotes

Money

Relationship

Wellbeing

Career / Education

Goals

Bucket List

Inspirational
Quotes

Money

Relationship

Wellbeing

Career / Education

Goals

Bucket List

Inspirational
Quotes

Money

Relationship

Wellbeing

Career / Education

Goals

Bucket List

Inspirational
Quotes

Money

Relationship

Wellbeing

Career / Education

Goals

Bucket List

Inspirational Quotes

Money

Relationship

Wellbeing

Career / Education

Goals

Bucket List

Inspirational
Quotes

Money

Relationship

Wellbeing

Career / Education

Goals

Bucket List

Inspirational
Quotes

Money

Relationship

Wellbeing

Career / Education

Goals

Bucket List

Inspirational
Quotes

Money

Relationship

Wellbeing

Career / Education

Goals

Bucket List

Inspirational
Quotes

Money

Relationship

Wellbeing

Career / Education

Goals

Bucket List

Inspirational
Quotes

Money

Relationship

Wellbeing

Career / Education

Goals

Bucket List

Inspirational
Quotes

Money

Relationship

Wellbeing

Career / Education

Goals

Bucket List

Inspirational
Quotes

Money

Relationship

Wellbeing

Career / Education

Goals

Bucket List

Inspirational
Quotes

Money

Relationship

Wellbeing

Career / Education

Goals

Bucket List

Inspirational
Quotes

Money

Relationship

Wellbeing

Career / Education

Goals

Bucket List

Inspirational Quotes

Money

Relationship

Wellbeing

Career / Education

Goals

Bucket List

Inspirational
Quotes

Money

Relationship

Wellbeing

Career / Education

Goals

Bucket List

Inspirational
Quotes

Money

Relationship

Wellbeing

Career / Education

Goals

Bucket List

Inspirational
Quotes

Money

Relationship

Wellbeing

Career / Education

Goals

Bucket List

Inspirational
Quotes

Money

Relationship

Wellbeing

Career / Education

Goals

Bucket List

Inspirational
Quotes

Money

Relationship

Wellbeing

Career / Education

Goals

Bucket List

Inspirational
Quotes

Money

Relationship

Wellbeing

Career / Education

Goals

Bucket List

Inspirational
Quotes

Money

Relationship

Wellbeing

Career / Education

Goals

Bucket List

Inspirational
Quotes

Money

Relationship

Wellbeing

Career / Education

Goals

Bucket List

Inspirational Quotes

Money

Relationship

Wellbeing

Career / Education

Goals

Bucket List

Inspirational Quotes

Money

Relationship

Wellbeing

Career / Education

Goals

Bucket List

Inspirational
Quotes

Money

Relationship

Wellbeing

Career / Education

Goals

Bucket List

Inspirational
Quotes

Money

Relationship

Wellbeing

Career / Education

Goals

Bucket List

Inspirational
Quotes

Money

Relationship

Wellbeing

Career / Education

Goals

Bucket List

Inspirational
Quotes

Money

Relationship

Wellbeing

Career / Education

Goals

Bucket List

Inspirational
Quotes

Money

Relationship

Wellbeing

Career / Education

Goals

Bucket List

Inspirational Quotes

Money

Relationship

Wellbeing

Career / Education

Goals

Bucket List

Inspirational
Quotes

Money

Relationship

Wellbeing

Career / Education

Goals

Bucket List

Inspirational
Quotes

Money

Relationship

Wellbeing

Career / Education

Goals

Bucket List

Inspirational
Quotes

Money

Relationship

Wellbeing

Career / Education

Goals

Bucket List

Inspirational
Quotes

Money

Relationship

Wellbeing

Career / Education

Goals

Bucket List

Inspirational
Quotes

Money

Relationship

Wellbeing

Career / Education

Goals

Bucket List

Inspirational Quotes

Money

Relationship

Wellbeing

Career / Education

Goals

Bucket List

Inspirational
Quotes

Money

Relationship

Wellbeing

Career / Education

Goals

Bucket List

Inspirational
Quotes

Money

Relationship

Wellbeing

Career / Education

Goals

Bucket List

Inspirational Quotes

Money

Relationship

Wellbeing

Career / Education

Goals

Bucket List

Inspirational
Quotes

Money

Relationship

Wellbeing

Career / Education

Goals

Bucket List

Inspirational Quotes

Money

Relationship

Wellbeing

Career / Education

Goals

Bucket List

Inspirational
Quotes

Money

Relationship

Wellbeing

Career / Education

Goals

Bucket List

Inspirational
Quotes

Money

Relationship

Wellbeing

Career / Education

Goals

Bucket List

Inspirational Quotes

Money

Relationship

Wellbeing

Career / Education

Goals

Bucket List

Inspirational Quotes

Money

Relationship

Wellbeing

Career / Education

Goals

Bucket List

Inspirational
Quotes

Money

Relationship

Wellbeing

Career / Education

Goals

Bucket List

Inspirational
Quotes

Money

Relationship

Wellbeing

Career / Education

Goals

Bucket List

Inspirational
Quotes

Money

Relationship

Wellbeing

Career / Education

Goals

Bucket List

Inspirational
Quotes

Money

Relationship

Wellbeing

Career / Education

Goals

Bucket List

Inspirational
Quotes

Money

Relationship

Wellbeing

Career / Education

Goals

Bucket List

Inspirational
Quotes

Money

Relationship

Wellbeing

Career / Education

Goals

Bucket List

Inspirational
Quotes

Money

Relationship

Wellbeing

Career / Education

Goals

Bucket List

Inspirational Quotes

Money

Relationship

Wellbeing

Career / Education

Goals

Bucket List

Inspirational Quotes

Money

Relationship

Wellbeing

Career / Education

Goals

Bucket List

Inspirational
Quotes

Money

Relationship

Wellbeing

Career / Education

Goals

Bucket List

Inspirational Quotes

Money

Relationship

Wellbeing

Career / Education

Goals

Bucket List

Inspirational
Quotes

Money

Relationship

Wellbeing

Career / Education

Goals

Bucket List

Inspirational Quotes

Money

Relationship

Wellbeing

Career / Education

Goals

Bucket List

Inspirational
Quotes

Money

Relationship

Wellbeing

Career / Education

Goals

Bucket List

Inspirational
Quotes

Money

Relationship

Wellbeing

Career / Education

Goals

Bucket List

Inspirational
Quotes

Money

Relationship

Wellbeing

Career / Education

Goals

Bucket List

Inspirational
Quotes

Money

Relationship

Wellbeing

Career / Education

Goals

Bucket List

Inspirational
Quotes

Money

Relationship

Wellbeing

Career / Education

Goals

Bucket List

Inspirational Quotes

Money

Relationship

Wellbeing

Career / Education

Goals

Bucket List

Inspirational
Quotes

Money

Relationship

Wellbeing

Career / Education

Goals

Bucket List

Inspirational
Quotes

Money

Relationship

Wellbeing

Career / Education

Goals

Bucket List

Inspirational
Quotes

Money

Relationship

Wellbeing

Career / Education

Goals

Bucket List

Inspirational
Quotes

Money

Relationship

Wellbeing

Career / Education

Goals

Bucket List

Inspirational
Quotes

Money

Relationship

Wellbeing

Career / Education

Goals

Bucket List

Inspirational
Quotes

Money

Relationship

Wellbeing

Career / Education

Goals

Bucket List

Inspirational
Quotes

Money

Relationship

Wellbeing

Career / Education

Goals

Bucket List

Inspirational Quotes

Money

Relationship

Wellbeing

Career / Education

Goals

Bucket List

Inspirational
Quotes

Money

Relationship

Wellbeing

Career / Education

Goals

Bucket List

Inspirational Quotes

Money

Relationship

Wellbeing

Career / Education

Goals

Bucket List

Inspirational Quotes

Money

Relationship

Wellbeing

Career / Education

Goals

Bucket List

Inspirational Quotes

Money

Relationship

Wellbeing

Career / Education

Goals

Bucket List

Inspirational Quotes

Money

Relationship

Wellbeing

Career / Education

Goals

Bucket List

Inspirational
Quotes

Money

Relationship

Wellbeing

Career / Education

Goals

Bucket List

Inspirational
Quotes

Money

Relationship

Wellbeing

Career / Education

Goals

Bucket List

Inspirational
Quotes

Money

Relationship

Wellbeing

Career / Education

Goals

Bucket List

Inspirational Quotes

Money

Relationship

Wellbeing

Career / Education

Goals

Bucket List

Inspirational
Quotes

Money

Relationship

Wellbeing

Career / Education

Goals

Bucket List

Inspirational
Quotes

Money

Relationship

Wellbeing

Career / Education

Goals

Bucket List

Inspirational
Quotes

Money

Relationship

Wellbeing

Career / Education

Goals

Bucket List

Inspirational
Quotes

Money

Relationship

Wellbeing

Career / Education

Goals

Bucket List

Inspirational
Quotes

Money

Relationship

Wellbeing

Career / Education

Goals

Bucket List

Inspirational Quotes

Money

Relationship

Wellbeing

Career / Education

Goals

Bucket List

Inspirational Quotes

Money

Relationship

Wellbeing

Career / Education

Goals

Bucket List

Inspirational Quotes

Money

Relationship

Wellbeing

Career / Education

Goals

Bucket List

Inspirational
Quotes

Money

Relationship

Wellbeing

Career / Education

Goals

Bucket List

Inspirational Quotes

Money

Relationship

Wellbeing

Career / Education

Goals

Bucket List

Inspirational
Quotes

Money

Relationship

Wellbeing

Career / Education

Goals

Bucket List

Inspirational
Quotes

Money

Relationship

Wellbeing

Career / Education

Goals

Bucket List

Inspirational
Quotes

Money

Relationship

Wellbeing

Career / Education

Goals

Bucket List

Inspirational
Quotes

Money

Relationship

Wellbeing

Career / Education

Goals

Bucket List

Inspirational
Quotes

Money

Relationship

Wellbeing

Career / Education

www.ingramcontent.com/pod-product-compliance
Lightning Source LLC
LaVergne TN
LVHW011730060526
838200LV00051B/3118
* 9 7 8 1 7 9 4 8 3 8 0 1 7 *